Bendigo

Fiona Cameron

NEWTON-LE-WILLOWS

Published in the United Kingdom in 2016
by The Knives Forks And Spoons Press,
122 Birley Street,
Newton-le-Willows,
Merseyside,
WA12 9UN.

ISBN 978-1-909443-78-5

Copyright © Fiona Cameron, 2016.

The right of Fiona Cameron to be identified as the author of this work has been asserted by her in accordance with the Copyrights, Designs and Patents Act of 1988. All rights reserved. No part of this publication may be reproduced, stored in a retrieval system, transmitted in any form or by any means, electronic, photocopying, recording or otherwise, without prior permission of the publisher.

Cover image: Jonathan Becker "Carriage, Paris," 1975.

For Emyr, Evan and Arthur

1

Bendigo means you want something urgently/command rushed through caverns of throat to air and reality in a flurry of frustration/bendigobendigobendigoBENDIGO!/pointing to a toy car just out of reach/then the tap/are you thirsty?/yes/tight fists grasp the mug/too rigid with determination to avoid the tilting slop and spill that comes when you move bodily with a drink/have you had enough to drink in this heat?/are we running out of milk?/need to buy

more at some point this
afternoon/note this/now
dinner thoughts/no, lunch
first/lunch first/ring
tone/message arrives in
another room/another
dimension/there's a bill
needs paying somewhere in
the back of my mind/tolling
like a dull bell at intervals
of varied panic/no time
now/no
time for this now/no
time

the cat appears like a spell

bendigobendigobendigo
CAT!/wow!/CAT!/radio
says that/

*at any one given moment
there are thousands of . . . /*

what?/kitchen cupboard
doors are wafting open and

shut/open and shut/creating
a balmy domestic wind and
out come all the pots and
pans/next/not the cutlery
drawer/no/no/no/stop/these
are sharp/let's make lunch
now/postman knocks/here
and gone long enough to
lose track of exactly where
we were headed/

**I know what's in this
package**

and now your nappy/open
first/the most immediate
package/halt this/lunch in a
little while/let's sit down
and do this calmly/a furious
windmill of limbs/play
interrupted for this?/

anguish streaks across your
tightening face like
lightening and then the tears
fall/hot face crossed by

salty tracks/every kick of
your legs striking a blow for
freedom denied/shrieks
rising higher/then/

oooohhhhh/you're still

the sun breaks out from
behind a cloud/the wind is
rising/the light has
altered/filter over
lens/*Mater Suspiria*/

lit for a film/the room is
glowing and instantly
distracted you watch the
trees dance at the
window/like you did at a
few weeks old/ shadows
beating/

the/walls/pupils/dilate in
wonder/you smile now/and
the change is
complete/release/

and to the bin/bin needs a
clean/there are nooks and
crannies here that disturb
me/their resistance to
relinquishing
filth/Domestos advert rings
in my head/your high chair
shows the crust of Weetabix

and parental guilt/

now lunch/but not from the
cat's bowl/no/no/no/let's
put that down/help me find
the bread and we'll make
cheese on toast/look, see
how the cheese grater
works/lunch is low on the
list/trailing far behind the
sudden urgent need to be
held/and your soft skin
brushes mine/twisting ropes
of my hair/

while the grill pulses and
heats behind us/

bee! bee! bee, mummy!/a
fly alights on the
windowsill geranium/ and I
lower you into the high
chair whilst you are
distracted/the cheese makes
contact with the bread/in
deft/swift moves it's under
and now it reconfigures
beneath the glowing
bars/NOOOOOOO/you say/
NOOOOO/and the hot melt
is rejected/cast down floor
wards with
grapes/cucumber/milk/

did babies in wartime do
this?/children ate everything
then didn't they?/

food is the first politics/
who said this?

no/babies are babies/we try
again/slowly this
time/approach with

caution/sip tea by your
side/window dream/in long
grass rushing sounds and
grand wind sweeps of the
old tree beyond the
window/window buts and
bangs somewhere in the
house/

the food is being eaten/*Déjà
vous*/my childhood sea
light/gulls cry 'alive'
outside/on the cusp of the
sky/I'm in Tarkovsky's
forests and your feet kick
my knees/hot mummy!hot
mummy!tea!/

I want to stand in the wind
and gulp air/

you reach insistent for my
mug/

*this is Winifred Robinson
with You and Yours*/

gently, it's still hot/you
inhale tea and exhale your
lunch remnants into the
swirl of tannins/pleased
with yourself/tea
mummy!hothothot/

*today we are discussing the
right to die. call or text now
on 844488/*

bendigobendigoBENDIGO!
/text message ping/not right
now/what is it
sweetie?/what did you
see?/bendigo/points in
several different
places/mentally scan the
worktop/more milk?/

**my eyes will locate your
words**

the bottle of chilli
sauce?/yes/hot/hot/hot/poet
h/poeth/poeth a different

sort of heat/its colour like
ketchup/there's no
difference to you/

*I watched my father die of
the same disease. I cannot, I
will not put my own family
through the same pain/*

dab chilli on my
tongue/ouch – look –
ouchy/*the discipline of
natural consequence* is what
my mother would have
called for in this
situation/hot/tears prick/

*you are flying to Zurich on
Saturday?/*

not 'dip dip'/hot hot/let's
put it away/would you like
some cake?/T'isho
cacen?/fly hits pane
repeatedly/bee/bee/bee/

now our next caller
disagrees with assisted
suicide/

CACENCACENCACEN!/

can you explain why?/oh
bloody text message
PING/you are quietly
stuffing chocolate cake at
speed into your mouth/eyes
brim with pleasure/

what is the Welsh for
PLEASURE?/

you laugh and laugh/
spraying cake across the
room/I dip my slice in
tea/feel the icing sugar
crystals melt/gaze at pattern
of food/strewn/at least three
times a day/brush and
dustpan/is ritual what keeps
you sane?/a curious
ritual/what would happen if

I stopped brushing up?/even
for one day/eye text
message now/*paddling pool
at ours this afternoon?/yes/I
think so/no/laughs/see you
2ish?/*

emails/quickly now/delete
junk/snapfishUKmatalannot
justalabelikeafamilyamazon
ukgrouponbootsoxfamcamp
aignsamnestychange.orgzuli
lyukevents/empty/slightlym
oreclearheaded/mummy?/

bendigobendigo/yes, let's
go/shall we tidy up first?/

*dying is part of life and who
are we, because I always
ask myself this, who are we
to decide the moment of
death?/*

right/let's get you
down/brush an avalanche of
crumbs from your t-

shirt/you speed off straight
into door jamb/momentary
silence/will you cry?/no/just
a bump/I say/YESH
YES/OK
now?/YESH/status
update/oh don't bother to
read this crap/clean up mess
first/I'm missing you/text to
tell you/package arrived for
you/DVD?/

Xavier Dolan/think so/he's
Rimbaud/

the evenings for our love

he's escape/can't wait to see
it/can't wait to see you/have
you done a poo?/no/ok/I
think you have/kitchen can
wait/come here/no
don't/don't touch that/ok/up
on my knee/let's have a
look/ nappy off/oh/no,
nothing/off you go/

*I'm going to have to stop
you there, we have other
callers waiting. Remember
844488 on the text or
hashtag
youandyours/tomorrows
phone in: buyer beware –
what's your opinion on the
'Big Six' energy
companies. . . ?/*

**sweetie, you *have* done a
poo**/I thought so/come
here/no/no/we need to do
this/can't go round all
mucky can we?/sat in front
of the window again/you're
examining a toy car
carefully/slowly spinning its
wheels/watching tiny tread
patterns/stroking the metal
work/absorbed/peace/

**I am outside under the
burning sky**

on an empty beach/gulls cry
again/WOW!wow!WOW!/s
eagull/I say/seagull/

*beep/beep/beep/beeeeep/thi
s is the world at one with
Martha Kearney/*

oooooohbeeeeeep/shush a
second
sweetie/beeeeeeepbeeeeepb
eeeeeeepbendigo/

*the latest ceasefire in Gaza
has collapsed after just four
hours/ reports from the
ground say casualties on
the Palestinian side now
exceed 130,000/*

I'm picking up crumbs

*most of the dead are women
and children/*

milk/white blank sky thick
like bandage/must buy
milk/no/no/no/no/no/no

nappy/it's all slow
motion/mind wanders out of
here/**hands do the
routine**/there's a dove in
flight in a childhood book/a
playing card tucked beneath
each wing feather/a cascade
of chance from the sky as
she turns/sky shuffle/sky
deals death/

let you down gently/watch
you run to the cat/toss her
carelessly/no, don't hurt her
baby/gently, she's only
little/she was
sleeping/silken pattern of
fur wriggles free/to another
room/make a bed
somewhere new/

*in other news Scottish First
Minister Alex Salmond goes
head to head with Alistair
Darling in a live debate on
Scottish independence
tonight/*

SHARE!!! you
scream/wrestling the used
nappy from my grip/no, this
isn't for sharing/yucky/to
the bin/

*they're all 'tartan
Tories'/White Heather Club
bastards/*

my Scottish grandmother's
words are suddenly with
me/but Granny, what have
the English government
ever done for you?/

*aye, don't talk to me about
that/it's workers together,
not nations apart/*

but granny it's not like that
anymore/everything has
shifted/

aye hen/AYE/HEN/human
beings have shifted/

bendigobendigobendigodak
adakadakadakashoesshoess
hoes/on now/on now/on
now mummy/wellies on the
wrong feet/stumbling to the
front door/

I am still in Scotland/at my
grandmother's feet/axe the
poll tax pin shines at me
from her Formica bedside
table all those years ago/it
was fluorescent pink and
angry text in black/where
are we now?/socialism in
Scotland gave my great
grandfather the strength to
turn the priest from his front
door/no wonder you're
holding on tightly/you're
fighting the lock on the
front door/

not yet sweetie/we need to
clear up lunch/here, let's
have TV for ten

minutes/*hello!hello!how are you?hello!hello!i'm happy to see you . . . well HELLO!*/OOOOH yesh/ten minutes and mummy will be done/giggles now/calm/kitchen/sunlit/a dirty battlefield/detritus/

a currency union is out of the question/Salmond does not have a 'plan b'/voters need to ask themselves exactly how he intends to secure fiscal stability . . . /

Cameron cemetery at Lochaline/a Cameron in every pit/I stood there for a long/ long time one summer/25/highland clearance/I can hear a phone ring/pop tones/prophetic/79/that's what English governance did for you/cheese ground

into lino/bleach/opaque
dead eyed fish/no
bleach/use some fucking
Ecover/

*what's inside Mr Tumble's
spotty bag today?/*

ooooooooh/we've got to
go/we've got to go/TV
off/scoop you up/and to
car/sun is scorching lines on
concrete/forcing its
will/wind down all
windows/

*on market square/we were
carried away/*

ETO/ETO/ETO/I read once
that Bukowski? started to
crave another cigarette
halfway through the current
one - he was that bad/you
are like that with songs in
the car/ETO/ETO/ETO

MUMMY!/ halfway
through/rampaging through
songs/always on repeat/I
know we can drive to
Bethesda in roughly six
plays of Duke/ 4 plays of
International Colouring
Competition/and 3 plays of
The Story of the Blues/car
time is not the same
anyway/is it?/

stretches/tides/recedes/song
feels different in
motion/wing span of the
bridge flies/flies/

**when the sunlight through
the suspension hits you in
stripes**

Gysin got there first

I watch your face in the
mirror/flicker book
emotions/so fast/changing
before my eyes/

will these moments ever make it to your adult narrative?

we landscaped our legacies and thought about wars

Sunday bells are tolling/for Scotland?/it's not Sunday/ I thought heard them once in the dead of the night/over the road/beneath the black yews/Tom's Diner/The Sensual World/in my teenage patchwork they are pricked/what use are nations?/pieces of dull similarity/bells herald the end/judgement/you're not the joining type are you?/any club that will have me as a member?/what is a nation anyway?/

As I'm listening to the bells of the cathedral/ I am thinking of your voice/

don't sleep now
baby/there's no point/

2

welcome to the pleasure dome

snigger/old joke/you live so high up/ a cradle of light upon the mountainside/ a lone tree makes the rule of thirds in your mind's eye/always/and the wind is always so high/you/it never calms down/ dust bowl/hillside/hideout/you are higher than the slate/maybe you aren't Bethesda at all?/the slate cannot colour you/does your Englishness sit apart up here?/from your look out?/

into your drive/still
sleeping/sweat pricking
your brow/and high red in
your cheeks/it's time to
come out/I start to wake
you/weak mewls as your
peace is broken/eyes
starting to
open/immediately changing
and appraising/frightened
cries now/as you assess the
unfamiliar/the unfamiliar is
intriguing/cries slow to
questioning sounds/no
words yet/no words/for
this/yet/

there is a night lantern
hanging in the lone tree/we
are in the foothills of the
Atlas mountains/mummy
drove you across continents
and crossed the sea/to bring
you to the Gwynedd
dustbowl/

Bendigo

where am I?/who am I?/I
slept across time and
culture/borne up
into/blinding sun high
courtyard/plunge
pit/paddling pool/full of
glistening/icy/mountain
water/phone shoved away
now/cannot disturb this
world/with another
world/inside a piece of
plastic/and the baby dances
around the pool/searching
for a way in/
testing the water with
fingers/toes/toys/under the
parasol/I thought about
escape/why you are
here/who are you
really?/you make
peppermint tea/we swirl
sugar and mint leaves
through it/like they do in
Africa/in the heat/you're
tired/fed up/sick of the day
to day/the discipline/the

reprimands/the lack of sleep/the constant/constant/constant/ sometimes I wake up and wonder how I'll get through another day/your sad eyes/sipping/telling me two times/of two recent times/

I look at the children in the pool/screeching in delight/a jangle of beaten sliver /your faces/ face/crumples/defeated/ as you talk/about the women/who can just do it/do it well/who are they?/manage 3 or 4/not me/I've lost my space/my mind/my peace/you say/and I wonder what your inner world is populated with/

inside of me is safe

nomad on the hillside/silken eared goats come to the

fence/the children feed them
grass from the garden/the
grass is longer in their
field/but they still come
here/to another being/an
interaction/I sit in the cool
of your bathroom/away
from the heat for a
minute/white prison
cell/washing my hands/I
look down upon the
garden/your head in your
hands/I bite my lip/women
socially policed in their
parenting/no wonder you
cry/they've told you you've
failed/don't buy it/get
angry/your home is full of
ideas/your mind is full of
ideas you've been sold/by
people who know/not a
thing/

wake up/please/wake
up/you are doing just
fine/go and bellow rebellion

into the crucible of the
mountains/don't hide away
up here/

down to the garden/we're
going to the river/this is
better/moving water/change
is bubbling/time moves at a
different pace/flushes
thoughts/here you are
happy/ier/babies amongst
the
rocks/absorbed/exploring/

**green pours over green
over green over green**

acid yellow mossy
seats/chalky flecked rock
tells us/seems to have a
heartbeat/in the
heat/thousands of
years/thousands of
children/mothers/felt these
waters/owed no one an
answer/ sat here/like

us/mould us/just try it/just
try it/just try it/and see how
far you get/

I think we drift away
now/school is calling/time
has ebbed up here/quartered
up by the divisions of the
bells/don't want to come
down from the
mountain/switch between
two worlds now/we're both
covered in mud/you and I/I
smile/roll up your
dungarees/nononononono
nomummy/nonononononon
onono/

it seems to me to shew an
abominable sort of
conceited independence

time to go sweetie/want the
school gates to see our
mud/see our time spent
elsewhere/not under the

bells/still here/though/say goodbye now/we need to collect your brother/YESH!YESH!/and tumble down the mountain on foot and then by car/all the way down/further and further to the road out/look back up and you're gone/a circle of burnt grass/a fleck, if that/a world encased in a fleck/something reflecting sunlight somewhere/shimmers momentarily/wobbles/in the hills/somewhere/

time

      is

            ticking

                  now.

3

'Tom at the Farm' is crap/we're both agreed on that/LET DOWN/adapted from the book/why do I need
to shout/I do/sometimes/volume makes up for the lack of order and the bad behaviour of words/in my head anyway/mind works too fast to scrabble for the words I need/in the morning/now/heat is rising again/cats calling for breakfast/windows slammed wide open/

*you're listening to Today
with John Humphrey's and
Mishal Husain/*

OH SHUT UP
HUMPHREYS/FOR
GOD'S SAKE/SHUT
UP!/he's not even got
started yet/let's tell him to
shut up before he
does/laughing and
laughing/oh Christ!/no!/not
the cornflakes/too
late/OK/let's try that
again/some toast
first?/YESH!/YESH!/NOO
OOOOOO!/YESH/smiles/jam
is magic/feed the children
SUGAR!/coffee ascending
in my
veins/right/about/now/

trapped time of day/good
for ideas/bad for time/try
and maintain mental storage
capacity/Azag/sky deals

death again/Azag/repeat
after me/REPEAT AFTER
ME/

*after last night's live debate
polls are now for the first
time placing the 'Yes'
campaign ahead of 'Better
Together'/good/James
Naughtie reports firstly
from the Isle of Skye in a . . . /*

no, no you are going to eat
what I put in these
sandwiches/I am not
making something different
for every single member of
this household/

notebook/pen/where?/noteb
ook/pen/list/you have your
lists/smile/you list daily/I
list when I am
panicking/smile/love/\love/

*Scotland's traditional
labour heartlands are*

where this battle will be fought/workers together, not nations apart/keeps gnawing at me/we don't care/nationalism/it's tricky one/can feel tensions rising/BBC need to forget who they think they are/on shaky ground as it is/forget that they ever ruled anything/only ever thought they did/post war/need to cling to something/was it misplaced desperate sense of empire?/we all fell asleep for a hundred years/all respect has died/no going back/it's all changed/sky cracked from side to side/windows closed again/a storm from nowhere?/I don't think so/it was a long time coming/

kissed you both goodbye/glass between us

till/6 o'clock/your confident shoulders/heft a happiness/I have never known before/I see the man in your childish face right now/flashes of future/floor me/as you walk away/and I see the boy in yours/everyday/everyday/everyday/

and now the dishwasher flashes its whites at me/a wall of steam/a washing machine full of sweet smells and all your little clothes/all the machines humming/working/turning time/

setting the next revolution of the wheel to tipping point

the next basket/the next dirty plate/the hours carved out in the decimation of

soap powder pots/in cat
litter spills and brush and
dustpan/making their
dance/across the kitchen
floor/they mark the minutes
the hours/the days/of our
lives/the frame/mime
washing your face when
your water has been taken
/never despise the
beauty/sanity of/ the
practical ritual/David's Last
Summer/floods my mind
with sound/why?/something
to do with the light/palms in
the abandoned glass
house/plant shadow dance/

and the whole world/the
dance of the domestic/Belle
and the Candlestick/a
conversation between
crockery/a knife drawer
fight/I shut the door and up
you come/let's go out/leave
the

cats/CATCATCAT!/wander
out of this house/into the
town/

no direction

just wait and
see/nappy/shoes/bag/poo
bag/you shout/poo
bag/huh?/poo bag
mummy/points/oh!/the
'pool bag'/swim bag!/well
done/da iawn babi/free
now/sky opens up again/a
song/shall we see where we
end up?/will you walk
today?/these skies don't
deal death/yet/only
seagulls/will this change in
your lifetime?/onwards
onwards towards the sea/no
mobile signal here/free/we
saw an adder here
once/danger in the
grass/disturbed soil/long
grass/dark forests/Europe/

no time to catch our breath

we all know what they conceal/it's not been dealt with/absorbed by minds that still can't carry this weight/before the next onslaught/before we plunge in all over again/storm is coming/there's a humming out at sea/in places we can't begin to imagine/

in-between the 140 characters

in between the snatches heard on the airwaves/spied through doors left ajar/words overheard at some midway hell point between Fflint and Birkenhead Central/

you immersed your baby's
head at the old church/two
weeks ago/and I never felt
so dead or so
empty/before/frightened for
you/I should have come in
wearing mud/there was no
point/nobody is listening
to/the pointless ritual
religion/of the fields/of the
corn/of death/we'll all go
down together/down to the
sea/you can always leave by
way of the sea/you can
always leave/even if you
swim to your death/your
dream of incarceration
frightens me/more in the
daylight/than in the
chamber of night/when it
spilled out/a night
reality/drowned in a prison
cell/anchored
ankle/thoughts are
clambering/clamouring in
queues/today/will the storm

break?/I sense no easy
answers for a while/

Bobby

    Shafto's

        gone

            to

                sea

plateau/and run right
through the night.

4

Morning crush/of toast/coffee machine gurgle/news/compelled to switch the radio on/radio on/it's him again/Alba/Yr Alban/being Scottish/uh oh!/uh oh!/uh oh!/you're splatting raspberries at the floor/hurling them like grenades/raspberry colour/like no other/explodes in scudding splash/Scottish Pineapple cake/ these came in raspberry flavour too/so it emerged/they appeared out of nowhere/like a bloom/ of pastel mushrooms/

new kitten sniffs at the
mess/her fur/and that/crush
of pink/would make a
glamourous coat/ah, it's
official/radio says
so/Gordon Brown has been
wheeled out/oh spare
us/please/Darling shoved
away somewhere/eyebrows
hushed/

*Gordon Brown is expected
to head the Better Together
rally today in Falkirk. The
question now is whether he
can . . . /*

he's the God fearing
Scot/dour man of the
manse/I can't work
out/what he wants us to
be/return to wide-eyed
terror of the peasant?/

**news of portents and
omens/fill September days**

The Mirror and The
Sun/scatter bad vibes/take
the form of/portentous
pasties/clouds/toast/showing up in the shape of a
decapitated/UK/

*Mrs Carpenter, 56, of
Tunbridge Wells saw the
end of the Union in her
morning croissant. She says
she's not one to usually put
much stock in these things,
but . . . /*

minus Scotland/bitten
off/vanished into thin air or
sea/sunk/forgotten/mystical
nation submerged/is that
what will
happen?/Ys/Scappa
Flow/don't look down
dear/the depths are
dizzying/

Fiona Cameron

**there's a nation down
there**

waving in the
trench/breakfast mess does
not divine/an answer for
me/I see in the raspberry
squash/wild raspberries
growing/winding on the
Ardnamurchan
Peninsula/reclaiming
ruins/growing
rampant/trampled
underfoot/sometimes/once a
century/if that/disturbed
only in times of greatest
need/no, don't eat them off
the floor sweetie/let's go
now/out on errands/off to
/Biwmares/

we're distracted by the
sea/and the heat haze
rising/and slow pebble
throw/in sleepy
movements/we're hardly

awake yet/you sit in the
waves/a wet bum by
9.30am/a sand covered
toddler enveloped in sea
mist/stately façade/hides a
hate/high street/spills a
collection of shops that sell
expensive things/to
expensive people/

buy things/non-essential items

women in charity
shop/tut/tut/tut/as you
scream in your buggy/out
and across the
shop/wreaking havoc/face
them down/then get you
out/glare back at
them/double necked
harridan hiss/follows us
out/already too hot
today/cross and
angry/desiccated
hags/seagull eyes you/in car

park/steals your biscuit/oh,
for god's sake!/cries bounce
around the courtyard/and
creeping winged
monster/hobbledy
hops/away with prize/blank
eyed/

let's go/into Bangor/over
the bridge/crossing the
water/you're sleeping
now/red faced/cross/about
the bird/my anger
abating/clutching list/pick
up flier/performance
tonight/Memorial Arch/1st
World War/projections/ of
what?/am
intrigued/Gordon's hotting
up/shouting now/in
Falkirk/turn radio down/try
not to wake you/

*when young men were
injured in these wars, they
didn't look to each other*

*and ask whether you were
Scots or English; they came
to each others' aid because
they were part of a common
cause. And we not only won
these wars together; we
won the peace together. We
built the health service
together. We built the
welfare state together.* ***We
will build the future
together***

silence now/sea sick/

wake you gently/stirring in
the heat/wander slowly
through town/we're more at
home here/you come down
on lunch break/we look at
THE BUILDING
together/it'll never be
finished/in time/we leave
you/

head to the library/sunken
children's
area/ergonomically
designed for you/bright
toys/chairs/tables/games/but
you decide/you will try and
dismantle the
photocopier/take the hooked
window pole down/

**swing it wildly like a
medieval warrior**

before we can catch
you/nearly taking out the
lights/me and the
librarians/disengage
you/body stiffens/writhes
from grip/screams tear
down the ceiling/echo
through the roof
vaults/bristling tension from
other readers/librarians
smile/tense/try and try again
to strap you into buggy/you
buck and

kick/scream/buck/kick/scream buck/kick/shoes off/ and thrown across the room/head down/concentrate/sweat prickles/force seat buckle to click/swing buggy out of here/we roll too close/to the magazines/you swipe/the lot/off the shelf/in one deft/angry move/so cross with me/bend to pick them up/ you swipe again/watching the words fly/and adjust you/ so you cannot reach/the words/

am turning in circles

to contain the destruction/now nothing within arm's reach/we leave/get out/smile stiffly/and close door/

get you to the car/other errands in town/abandoned/food shop is essential/**can.do.this**/just one of those days/babies are as changeable as any adult/you are just having a cross day/I need to calm down/of course you hate being constrained/we leave to walk on the island/water is so high/full moon?/new moon?/swelling upwards/shimmering and spilling/autumn afternoon/lit through the trees/we walk and run/collect acorns and leaves/just one of those days/you trip up a lot/cry a lot/want/then don't want/snatch/then discard/then cry/I hug you tight/just one of those days/

we have to shop/I am
convinced we can do this/if
we remain calm/trolley
seat/no/carry/no/hold my
hand/no/sit in trolley
basket/no/explosion of
limbs/scream/at a pitch/high
enough/to elicit winces
from other shoppers/move
quickly now/keep your
interest/distract you/see
those carrots?/help mummy
out/ put them in the
bag/hurled across the aisle/I
force you into trolley
seat/and strap you in/grit
teeth/you're pulling at
strap/ripping at
it/screaming/desperate arms
swipes/at anything in
sight/toiletries aisle/sends a
shower of bottles crashing
floor-ward/strap has come
undone/you're trying to
stand up on seat
now/reclaim your

independence/wobbling/res
eat you/to shower of fresh
screams/**am.that.close/**

parents have abandoned
trolleys mid-shop/get to
check-out/too near
conveyor belt/you grab
again/someone else's
shopping heading floor-
ward/intercepted/moved
outwards/now too close to
opposite queue/and you
grab at a man's jacket/he
swings round/angry darting
eyes/tears finally prick in
mine/

**the unkindness of other
people**

try and navigate a middle
space while we wait our
turn/you bite into a
lemon/in anger/horror
face/hurled again/bag up

this shopping/quickly out to
car/breathe/have forgotten
half of what we went in
for/you watch me/for a
moment/expectantly/then
rip a banana from a bag and
throw it at the car
windscreen/the last straw/an
absurd/and hilarious action
of defiance/I find myself
laughing and
laughing/shoppers
watch/Jesus/full moon/I'll
blame the full moon for all
of this/slowly get your
perspective back/I tell
myself/mater suspiria/just
one of those days.

We go online/later/to see
what the performance
looked like/projections on
an unfinished building/the
flickering faces of all those
local dead boys/illuminated
against a monolith/an

incomplete art house/and
Gordon is still shouting
about our union of
death/decapitated nationalist
croissants fill my head like
clouds/it's late now/

sleep is seeping

see a cavernous
doorway/something in
there/am rocking you to
sleep/your sleep is
catching/I can feel myself
slipping/the arc of your
eyelash line/flutters/rapid
movement beneath/sun dies
behind the curtains/your
body slackens/at peace/at
last/all anger abated/I slip
out/and click your door
shut/and wander to the hall
window/watch the traffic
for a while/lights blinking
on now/moon
rising/christening returns to

me/why?/glittering
font/dead ritual/slowly
make my way downstairs/to

**The Sound of Young
Scotland**

**dream to the image of
perpetually arriving at a
locked gate**

just one of those days.

5

Words have arrived today/like a long delayed train

with them/comes a sense of calm/a release of tension from your body/it really does happen like this/overnight acquisition/the words are in free flow/parroting everything back at me/as if it had always been this way/you smile and smile/knowing you have broken through something important/no wonder the anger raged in torrents of frustration yesterday/

the radio tells me we're
being taken to war again/
via the back
door/slowly/slowly/edging
closer/like an ill-fitting pair
of jeans/forced to fit the
chubby thigh/

**this war is going on/so
help me god**

even if I can't get the zipper
up/maybe if I lie down/and
squeeze myself in this
way?/d'you reckon anyone
will notice?/you don't fool
us/you don't fool anyone
anymore/perpetual
warring/it's become our
only
language/Oceania/Eurasia/
Eastasia/it's happened right
before our stupid
eyes/Scotland could choose
to have no part in
this/Scotland could choose a

lot of things/I worry silently
that nationalism stinks/it
always does/

*The Iraqi Government have
requested Western
intervention in the fight
against/ISIS/ISIL/ISLAMIC
STATE/*

blah blah/Obama thinks we
have a duty to be in
there/only in the sense we
caused the mess in the first
place/they really can't
see/today is shaping up to
be a stormy day/we're alone
in the house now/singing to
ourselves/humming
pathways around the
rooms/tidying as we
go/picking up books and
chattering/I switch the radio
off/because Women's Hour
has started/the wind is
picking up outside

now/suddenly feel very
cosy/the cats are
sleeping/and you lay across
the blanket/touching their
fur/cooing to
yourself/opening and
closing your mouth/shaping
sounds/shaping
words/shaping your
language/your
expression/these sounds are
for you alone/lapping
gently/

**moon!/you cry
suddenly/moon!**

the day time moon is
apparent in the
window/moon!/you say it
with such emotion/you own
the moon now/that you can
say it/

thinking about words/neud
nid deud/the radio is
strangled in an excess/a glut
of words/with no
purpose/indulgent and
destructive words/maybe as
a nation we just talk too
much/intellectualise our
emotions/so we'll never
act/sleepwalking with a
chatty narrative/everyone is
just winging it all the
time/keep talking/don't
stop/in the silence/we'll
discover the truth/time is
running out/words get faster
and louder/as deadlines
approach/time speeds up/

**then falls to an
aching/stretching stream
of low guttural moans**

just because you are
speaking/does not mean you
can be heard/you could be
screaming for all they care/

*do so in defiance not only of
the Westminster consensus
but also of its enforcers: the
detached, complacent
people who claim to speak
on their behalf/*

the golden circle/we feel so
far away/so tiny
sometimes/but
sure/Fotheringay/all the
same/when your time has
come/I am watching the egg
timer/carefully/your lunch
is constructing itself/bread
under the grill/becoming
toast/redefining itself in
front of my eyes/when it
emerges the salty butter
slicks on in slow motion/I
imagine the knife/will stand
up tall/in the cutlery
drawer/step out and stoop to
the job/quick/back/forth/and
off to the sink/the egg is
changing too/timing it on

my phone/but pull it before
the ringer tells me to/I know
it's how you want
it/because sometimes you
can just tell/and I am
right/every action in the
kitchen is slowing down to
glowing seconds of clear
light/sometimes I like
having a head cold/because
it stops my mind from
whirring/slows the thought
process down/today/this has
happened because of the
light/the wind/the growing
sense of anticipation oozing
from radio/seeping in the
ether/present you with egg
and soldiers/EGG!/you
shout/EGG!/

*this is Winifred Robinson
with Call You and Yours*/

maybe I really should just
stop listening to this/

*our first caller is the
daughter of the lady we
spoke to last week on our
programme about assisted
suicide. We've had a
massive response from
listeners who heard her
speak/*

is there nobody who will
take responsibility?/Brand
calls for insipid celebrity
revolution via the pages of
The Guardian/about as
revolutionary as wood chip
wallpaper/dipdipdipDIPDIP
EGGEGG/cheese and
cucumber
too?/YESH/NO/throws
cucumber at my
head/rearrange the set
up/OK, let's concentrate on
the egg/on the matter in
hand/half shutting my ears/

yes, mum flew to Zurich as planned on Saturday and she died with all her family around her/do you stand by her decision?/yes/yes/yes/I do/but I want her back so much/ . . . /

you are eating the eggshell

extract the river of shell and saliva/give you a drink of milk/we move onto yoghurt and fruit/move from seat to floor/to sofa/to stairs/to cot/to bed/to bathroom/climb onto shelf in our wardrobe and watch/me change the beds/tunnel in the duvet/COME IN!/you shout/COME IN!/

we're under here/under a crotchet blanket/watching outwards/faces flickered by

holes/in our cave/you feel
safe/you've made your first
den/your first home/we sit
with the teddies and the
books/watching and
tickling/we could be
anywhere in the world I
think/a den in the mountains
or the forest/deep under the
sea/

far deeper in space and
time/a capsule/when your
brother pretends to blast
you off in a tiny capsule to
the depths of the galaxy/I
sometimes half believe
you've been and made that
journey/floating in
blackness/curled in a ball/

waiting to arrive/unfurl

turning circles in
nothingness/

*through night and day and
in and out of weeks/*

and you won't know your
destination until you
arrive/don't alight here for
too long/this world is falling
down now/

and for the first time in
weeks/it starts to rain/heavy
and gusting/hard against the
bedroom window/our den
wobbles/the rain is hitting
the windowsill/the radio is
chattering far
away/downstairs/our little
blanket nation closes its
ears and eyes/in just a few
days time we could be
going it alone/

*if I hand someone ma
housekeeping money and
they make a mess of ma
house. I wanae take it back*

*and do it ma'self/that's all it
is hen, ya ken?/*

is it?/is it more than this?/is
identity linked to control?/

*if we are better together,
why aren't we better
together now?/*

said someone's comment
deep in the bowels of
Facebook/nobody listened
anyway/

and then you are sick

an unheralded torrent/across
you/me/the bed/the
floor/trying to stem the
flow/cupping my hand
beneath your mouth/why do
mothers do this
instinctively?/your face is
grey/the den/through the
holes of crotchet/confused
sobs/and shaking/we try and

navigate a way out of the mess/towards hot water/shower/fresh clothes/but it comes again/en route/no!/you cry and cry/no!/mummy no!/a lot can happen in the space of minute/day needs re juggling now/no school run/alternatives must be found fast/you smell of soap now/wet hair/dried carefully/soft pyjamas/blanket/sofa/sick bowl/you fall asleep/and I move quickly to sort the carnage in the bedroom/when I'm done/I'm back with you/on the sofa/waiting/listening to the whir of the washing machine/going full pelt now/the seconds stretch to hours/as I watch every movement of your sleeping face/the wind is gusting at

the window/and the
afternoon sun is trying to
breakthrough after the
storm/

I stare at the window for an
hour or more/who
knows/because this is the
first time I have sat still for
more than ten minutes in a
long time/and my thoughts
are confused/because they
are not sharing space with
another/

In

    the

        gap

            of

sickness

there comes calm and
reordering/I step over the

border of the windowsill/into the air/to walk on thin air/to dance upwards/to skate in a circle/to turn in the arc/to swoosh in the decay/to stand under the trees and tip back my head/tip back so far/I'm going to fall/like a child/to lose balance/and lie still and silent/watching the insects in the grass/to create the garden empire/the palace of leaves/the vistas of an imaginary land/populated only by ambition and dreams/it's all still there/stronger than ever/access only granted in certain circumstances/

and over days now/because time has changed for the purposes of this interlude/we're moving in a special sort of way/

**we're moving to the
febrile beat of sickness**

changes you and me/changes the rhythm of our life/a holiday in another time zone/normal service will be resumed/you are poorly for several days/and in that time/we wash more bed clothes/blankets/cushions/clothes/than I can remember/we all sleep together/we'll tenderly wrap you in the Dunvegan faerie flag/wakeful in a moonlit night/listening to you breathe/time passing by aside invisible night clouds/Scotland/

**and I dream/about
childhood sickness**

in Scotland/age five/deepest
night/ awake in a caravan
overlooking Faslane/all
were sleeping/the
lighthouse beam at
intervals/kept me
company/and I saw the dark
mass of a submarine/rise
once/break the surface of
the black water/in the
moonlight/you breath in the
darkest part of the water/
I thought I must have been
the only person on earth that
night/alone with a
newborn/night on earth/my
secret/and day
breaks/shining sheets of
light across our room/

arise to Sir Evan Davies and
Sir Justin Webb/grave
tones/serious business all
this/suddenly/simpering
cacophony of cross party
unity/as vows are now

being pledged/hollow
sentiments/if we were a
socialist UK/independence
wouldn't be an issue/isn't
that the truth?/really?/fear
being driven steely eyed
and hard-nosed/the
vow/isn't a vow/it's a
promise to
themselves/concocted by/a
morally bankrupt PR agent
somewhere in a
Westminster hole/

*oh yes, the whole debate in
Scotland has certainly fired
up an interest in politics
again. A little anecdote: this
week I was in a Glasgow
city centre pub when a
rowdy hen party came in
and what were they talking
about? The Barnett
Formula . . . well . . . there you
go. Who'd have thought?/*

thought what exactly?/do explain yourself/simultaneously cringing and diving for the off button/Victorian values at the BBC/something, time and tide can't seem to change/I want to swim today/I want to dive far far down and surface somewhere else/through a white tiled tunnel/lit by the moon underwater/I used to think Scotland was where you went to escape/a place/other/to hide/to become untouchable/I checked you out online/but the Google car doesn't go that far/

the bits I want now/are gone.

6

Will today be the day?

it's the eighteenth day of September 2014

sickness is passing/lemon light and weak tea/wan and pale/sort of day/and I just kind of know/now/this day will collectively stretch like an elastic band/and slap right back on our wrists/stinging for a long while/maybe it was a sickness/of sorts/this is a slow close to delirium/a resurfacing/all is a dream/I am watching the

interminable line/the riding
of waves/of the polling
station queue/something so
regimental/does the very
communal/lonely act of
going to vote/make you
different/to your hopes and
dreams/

on a snowy hill/we rose
up/climbed to the tree lined
summit/leaned for a
while/and saw/it all below
us/described how we would
descend/how we would end
our story/and in the distance
the church called/bells rang
out across the valley/siren
to our drowning souls/it's
an end/of sorts/answers
should be clear in the
crystalline snow light/but
they are no clearer now/than
they ever were/we're all of
us/

just winging it/every day

because this bubble of a few
weeks/has now occurred
before my eyes/because
when I hold you/and dare to
imagine the horror of
learning to unleash a future
we don't control/we
unravel/there are no
borders/our inner dreaming
is our only reality.

**and the doctor finally
came at dawn**

and I know the
answer/don't have to ask/his
ashen face/for sure/and turn
to the blue light face of my
phone/ to confirm the
time/not the answer/I know
I won't wake you/you've
already worked this one out
for yourself/we all/already
know what the answer
is/always will be

time warps and forgets/in a
week/it'll all be gone/rush
of water through the
reservoir/deep/deep/down/fi
zzing with
energy/dissipating against
the rocks/onto the next

problem

*onwards and
upwards*/Hague says
Westminster will be held to
account/

**can no longer dodge the
issue**